3

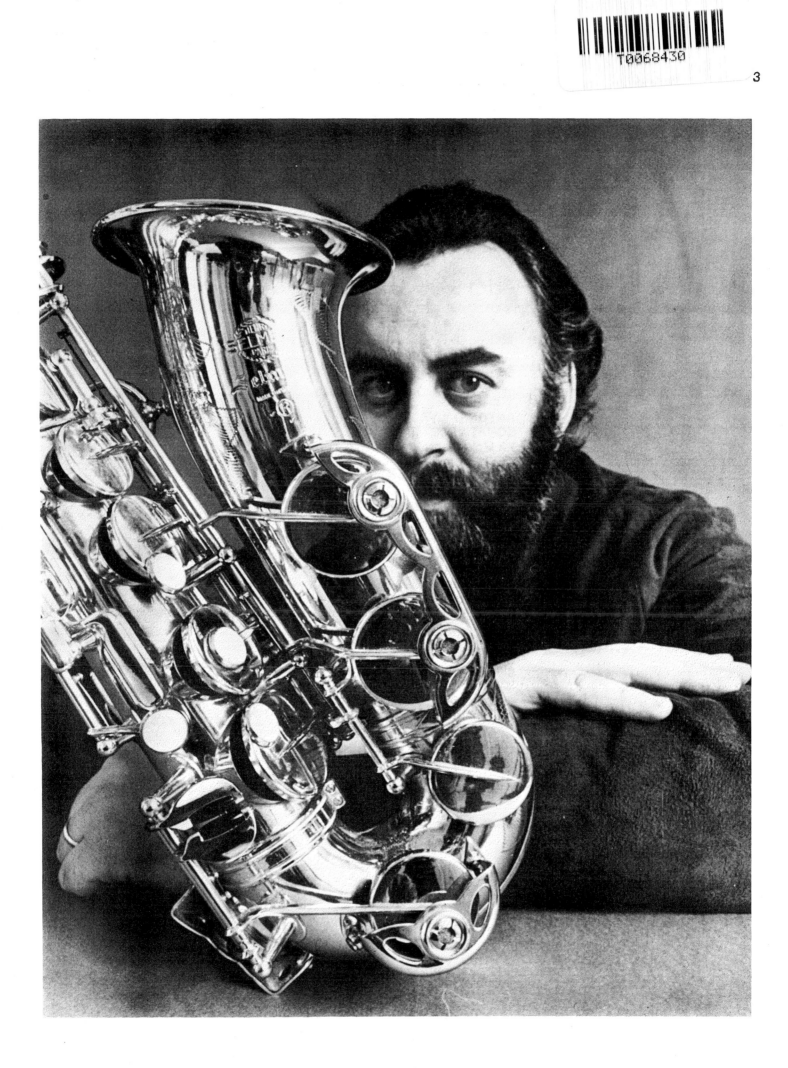

ALTO SAXOPHONE MUSIC

TUNING

Before the piano accompaniment begins you will hear four tuning notes, followed by a short scale and another tuning note. This will enable you to tune your instrument to the record.

SONATA NO. 6 IN G MINOR

I

Side A - Band 8 ♩. = 56 (1'08")
3 Beats Precede Music

ANTONIO VIVALDI
Arr. by Erwin Bodky

8027

Side A - Band 9 ♩ = 104 (1'56")
3 Beats Precede Music

Fuga da Capella

8027

8027

III

Side A – Band 10 ♪ = 66 (1'46")
3 Beats Precede Music

IV

Side B – Band 2 ♩ = 112 (2'28")
Side B – Band 3 ♩ = 76 (3'24")

4 ♩ precede music

8027

8027

8027

AN ABSTRACT

DAVID WARD

Side B - Band 4 ♩= 72 (3'34")

Side B - Band 5 ♩= 96 (2'50")

8027

8027

SONATA

Side B – Band 6 ♩· = 104 (3'28")
Side B – Band 7 ♩· = 96 (4'16")

WOLFGANG JACOBI

4 ♩ precede music

Allegro, ma non troppo

8027